CHIASMA

Paul Goepfert

Panjandrum Books, Inc.
Los Angeles   San Francisco

Parts of this poem have appeared in the magazine: *Low Company*.

First printing: August 1, 1980

Manufactured in the United States of America.

Graphics: Bruce Skogen.

Library of Congress Cataloging in Publication Data

Goepfert, Paul, 1945—
   Chiasma.

   I. Title.
PS3557.O322C47   811'.54   79-27133
ISBN 0-915572-39-7

This book was made possible in part by a grant from
The National Endowment for the Arts, a Federal Agency.

Further inquiries should be directed to:
Panjandrum Books, Inc.
11321 Iowa Ave., Suite 1
Los Angeles, California 90025

"In reality there is neither me nor the other as positive, positive subjectivities. There are two caverns, two openesses, two stages where something will take place—and which belong to the same world, to the stage of Being. There is not the For Itself and the For the Other. They are each the other side of the other. . . . Chiasm is that: the reversibility. . . . The chiasm, reversibility, is the idea that every perception is doubled with a counter-perception, is an act with two faces, one no longer knows who speaks and who listens. Speaking-listening, seeing-being seen, perceiving-being perceived circularity (it is because of it that it seems to us that perception forms itself). . . . for me it is no longer a question of origins, nor limits, nor of a series of events going to a first cause, but one explosion of Being which is forever. Describe the world as rays of the world beyond every serial-eternitarian or ideal alternative—posit the existential eternity—the eternal body.

–Maurice Merleau-Ponty
The Visible and the Invisible

This poem has been taken from a longer series of poems which were written in first draft during a year that I lived and worked in Mexico and traveled in Guatemala, Honduras, and Belize.

Although this text, *Chiasma,* is accessible within itself, it was not initially intended as a book apart from this series; and it is within the development of that series that it is most variously readable.

However the extended length of the full series and my own hesitancy to bring it to premature closure has precluded the publication of the complete piece at this time. Pa'lante, poco a poco.

Only years later
able to say
dedicated to

      you   Karen
      this despite
      for the mode of
      this given   in
      and taken   for
      le don   granted
      so early   mythos of
      the body beside   love
      light in which to
      a   wake   new
      primitive

   dedicated to
   reverses
   to rhyme with....

The cymbal above
   all else   a sound
so shrill   so out of
time   and beyond
the tune   it begins
to recess in the flesh

sounding   as the nerves
in cicada swarmings
seven summers past   were
contrapuntal to a physical
thought of exteriors
but sounding as a silence

shrilling continuo
within the crashing
of the blood pulse
from the inside
out of the ear
I hear again

While here the eye sees

where dancers all day
become their masks
with perfect gestures

Los Christianos y Los Moros
reenact   enact   and prophesy

and here where I appear   most   out of the crowd
with a sudden blow   a closure of hands
a blessing   some how   in a girl's hands

holding my face   I am   holding her face
touching   the perfect gesture
mnemonic   to webs   I am
crysalis still
born of this other   sign and flesh in
the frame of eyes   the shrill insect air
brought taut to this cymbal

as hands   touched   by fret
of thought in silken threads
lay upon and beyond
the silence in the sound

The first utterance
is a gift
then a debt

I must answer
and to which yet
an other responds

With scripts even to the tips
of our hands outstretched
to the contours of the actual
lost in a crowd of images
lost in a crowd of words

While the dancers gladly give
the gift of their names and faces

as their feet lift and their hands
swing down thru arcs of scimitars
they let go their lives
into this power adorned in silk

whose delirium is of the cymbal
whose speech is of the drum
and bugle and marimba
whose sight is of the animal eye
glazed within the garish mask

But mine is contoured
to a crowd of its own
images   warp   as if around
the eye   natal water was breaking

     beneath the garish mask
this other mask
I am still with   to weave
after so much time and space
holding   as the hands can
     cup a grail off
a young woman's face
     the image

of her   and then him
who was   I am still
     outside in
the frame of eyes
     the mask
          dicephalous

The music scaled
     on silken webs
          a rondo
               for the four hands
how it comes   around again
     for this   diver
               gent dance
          a fugue
how the mind goes
          to flee
          at once
vertical   and   horizontal
     polyphonies
          return
               differ
                    entially
     by lapse
from amnesia
     to amnesia
          alter
               nately
                    un able
to remember
          or to forget

I remember
with this cymbal shrilling
a deafness to my ears:
        straining to listen
        even as we talked
        how within that other
        shrill sounding of a thick
        summer's night   there was
        a change of pitch and timbre
        from dusk to dawn:
            another sound   not quite
            a silence   like a lapse
            from tinnitus to tinnitus
            modal to a thought
            of interiors:

            the hum of a swarm
            of cicada killer wasps
            punctuated by the song
            full frenzy of feeding birds

O ut of it   I think   I am
                drinking pulque among
        the crowd of indios
        home for the fiesta
        with a handful of wage
        from the canefields
        of the lowland valley

        Hiding out   I think   I am
        from the drone of progress
            down the pan american highway
            out from the capital
            out from Cuernavaca
            out on the barrio edge
        of Tepoztlan   beneath
        La Montana de Espuma

the green cataract cliffs
and the ruins of the temple
for the god of pulque
    Tepoztecatl

    Octli   They called it
when the milksap of maguey
mother Mayahuel   was a
breast of water for
nomads from the desert
a child or a fish
suckling her in the glyph
    and fermented it
    with roots of Ocpatli
        the pulque medicine
        to cure it   to wash
        away the poisons
        from the body
    public for
    the sacred days

Ce Malinalli   one grass
glyphed of calavera   skull
with spear-point grass

glyph of life in a snap

all that blooms early
and as quickly dies
as this first to seed
first to wither
rope-cord summer grass

as quick as   fermented for
the drunkard's deathly spree
of Ometochtli
el Dos Conejos
Day of Two Rabbits
    lord of the pulque
        master of the music
            and spieler of games

whose face was the blood stain
across the changeling moon
their wives kept watch with

whose death was the sleep
of too much pulquero dancing
in the fifth cup of drink
                he arose out of   alive
                from the maguey pit
                having puked   pissed   and shit
                all the poisons away
                by mid morning   next day
                or year   ready to begin
                all over again
                like corn in the spring

So they made the new fire
and fermented pulque for him
when the sun was gone south
and they were cutting
the harvest of corn
like heads from the necks
of drunken   captive men
        it was that sacred
            dangerous
                and they were
                    circumspect
in its use   only the old ones
for the washing
of the body of memory
the water of their tears
                and the daring ones
who would go dancing
swinging hatchets of copper
singing songs
            unto their perfect deaths
        were allowed to
            transgress
                with this excess
La Quinta Copa   they still call it

but now we all are
well into   our fifth cup
Ometochui   Rabbit-faced
shit-faced   we'd call it
piss drunk and dancing
and lighting off los cuetes
                        (cuetear   colloquially
                        locally   speaking
                        to kick   the bucket
                        to be so drunk
                        to explode
    as they will
                        these fireworks

thruout the night
to hear   they say
the voice of the mountain
speak out of time
echoing to remind
the old ones   of first loves
and first deaths   touching
hands   huddled in corn cellars
beneath the booming of Carranza's guns

They say
when a man has died
in drunkenness   the fault
into which he fell was
the fifth cup   an excess

like the cesspit
    where that old   man
they say
        stumbling
                died
having to swallow
    all the poisons passed
        from the whole
            of the body   public

like the fifth direction
of the metaphysicians
an abyss   an excess   even
Quetzalcoatl   the culture
bearer   the sower of flowers
in song   fell into with a fifth
cup of pulque for his sickness
unto death   from the Lord of
the Smoking Mirror of contradictions:
        could not forfend
        by any measure
        of boundary to the city
        or penance to the flesh
                against his twin of nature
                his own monstrous double
                of drunkenness   incest
                and scapegoat death

It is written
        (marginalia to the glyph of Tepoztecatl
        in the codice Magliabecchi de Florencia)
that when a man of this place
died in his drunkenness
the men would dance
as the daring ones did
the pulque drinking
Jaguars and Eagles
in two lines converging
with copper hatchets clanging

Thus the name of this place
Tepuztli   Axe of copper
tlan   of this place
I am not
                I am out of it
                step turn and time
                in this dance
                touching hands
                in homespun
                going the wrong way
                in a circle
                round faint embers
                their stories
                to warm me
                retrograde
                to my memory
                of hands
                in silken threads
                to tangle pale roots
                from a mask
                for the animal eye
                I am
                        out of it
                        Coneja   she says
                        twitching her nose
                        Cicada   I say
                        but returning
                        the gesture   despite
                        the insistent cymbal

                a riddle of eyes
                they allow me
                in my fifth cup
                as they turn me about
                as if to unravel
                me like a man
                sized medicine bundle

                    or to my own tune
                    turning   more thru less
                    as if unwinding
                    a swathe of sweat
                    shop silken swaddling

               that some image of my place
               might fall out from these tropes
               I am sounding   Cicada
               spinning   and I mean her
               but the whole   weave of the cloth
               spindle spinning   Cicada

                    but the bright silver pesos
                    are flying from my pockets
                    and it brings the whole
                    dance down   stopped
                    and staring at the dirt

     as if   of a sudden   some
     thing they know   a threat
     to their   value of use
     my distant name place
     assigns me to them
     this thin   insignia
     of exchange

     But not so out of it
     since they will not stoop
     to it   but only stare
     until I declare   de facto   it
     libre   I buy   drinks all around
     that the music might begin again
     that I might   be of that use

     But the young man with dull
     silver fingers insists
     on his gift in exchange:
     a high caliber magnum
     cartridge shell with crude scores
     cut for the image of a face
     into the cupreous colored lead

     He's no dirt farmer   he says
     brewing pulque in a piss pot
     he drinks   comemorativo tequila
     like the star   Aguilar   in the ads
     and works thirty k's down the road
     at the Remington Arms
     bullet packing plant

His voice is lost
in a hum of wasps
as the cymbal   again
shatters the air

and I am beside
myself in this   silence
of all that is   sounding
the depth of a cicada swarming night

    still humming
    coming from outside
    a kitchen window
    inside   Bucky Power's house

    where she and I   first
    assayed our talk   for bond
    of what   in the instance
    the flesh   unable   knew better

        twisting our necks
        in the park
        to look again   to
        each other for   that looking

recognition
our exclusive agitation
apart   from the dancing party
a mute fascination   mastered
to a dissemination   of talk

a fallacy   of words   to seduce
begging the question of
what the others would   then say
for an image   of the shopper's   cliche

was   love at first sight

was   our precipitin gage
like to like at first   like
to other at last   in
either equation   how even

sleep storied with   the social
unknown   what was   misrecognition
talked up from desire keeping
what down from desire   for what

    other   between us was irritation—

yes   tho bred into signs   more
primitive   yet   left to
imitation   with no story
to say   inherited   in the privy
flesh   the itch and scratch   again
st a made world   natura
lized   per omnia saecula saeculorum—

was always also   towards   What?
unwinding   this blindfold swathe
of sweat shop silken   swaddling

This bond of talk then   as it was
against the others   who
had enthroned us in our cliche
was one   rivalrous ŋeolithic thought:

decoding the youthful romance
for visions of distant places
and versions of self importance

that we would rise up out of
what they would sink down into
that small sub urban town

set smugly on edge with
what we had learned   in lieu
of   the story   for a place there
among the clapboard and brick ramshackle
defunct mill town-swamp-flats   of Jersey
to call   generically   the poor

was also   following
its own logic   finally
as double   bound as we
were both   of and not
of a place   there
as much against   as
for each other

We couldn't have known it
having listened to nothing
else for so long we were deaf

but walking out   for
the silence of the cool   dark
assuming the swarm   had passed

we never heard   a sound
until we stepped   down   flesh
exposed   smack into

the stinging   insect blast

hile the dancers gladly give
the gift of their names and faces

           "Ixtli-   a face"
           to be assumed
           "and by extension
           the eye"   focused to
           sites of namings
           in the mirror
           of the Tlamatini

   wise man   teacher
   of the faceless from
    birth   by citation
      to owners   of
       a proper face
   person of the tribe
   an eye   apparition
           of sight   for first dis
           tinction   "Tezcatlan
           extia-   in
           the mirror which
           illumines things"   Ubi
           quitous   transcendent
           signifier

       Ometeotl
     the first naming
   double   god   thing
     male and female
         initiates
  the oppositional sons
  the dance of   semiotics

           in two lines converging
           with copper hatchets clanging

how the gestures   all
so speak out of time

           as the dancers   keep time
           sutured along the seams

of their garish masks   the lines
of the dancers converging

                                        and falling away   their swords
                                        clanging   cut both ways   the time

of the air of this enact
ment of themselves   the time

                                        of the body   of their memory
                                        prefigured   paradigm   raveled

Abiding
                                                        beside themselves

    with wearing
                                                the mask of the

        Gachupin
                                        they go dancing
            as glazed white
                                faced christians
                with the golgatha
                    god's beard
                    They go dancing
            Abiding
                                inside themselves
        with wearing
                                        the mask of the
            desert moor

                                            they go dancing
        as glazed black
                                                faced islamics
with the prophet's
                                                    scimitar eye

        They go dancing
                                    beating their swords
                                    to the rhythm of the drums

until the battle's end
comes   again and again

                    the christians

                                    grinding   their barefoot heels
                                    beside the moors' lowered heads

                    over and over

they'll soon start again
each giving over

                                    their blood to the hours
                                    of the power that has seized them

and whose dance they will scribe
in the dust with their blood

In some like wise
        the alien   the prisoner
of the war of the flowers
learned the refinements
and sweet speech of the lords
of the calpulli   Became

ensigned   of the god   Blue
Hummingbird   or Wind with Rain
thru the months of ease
tutored among love songs
to flower in four women
for four directions   who forever
would entrance his pleasure
to the tropes of the sky
by the masks of a goddess
whose corn skulled girdle enclosed
entrance to sweet abyss
of the fifth direction

as he would wear
and become the mask
with perfect gestures
of the Teotl
of the "some
one's some
thing else"
of the Great Speaker
of the god
of the image
made from the fine dough
of crushed amaranth seeds

as he would dance
intoxicated with
Datura y Pulque
the Xochi power
of the sun   mask
into his body

arms opened with panicle
of plumeria petals for the sun
caught in the eagle's claw
where water of panthers
pours from the exposed roots

                        (though then as now
                          as like to like
                            is like wise
                              other
                            it would be
                              only
                               he
                             for all
                          the rest he was
                        beneath the ultimate
                        blue blade   who was
                    rived from sternum to groin
                      torn   into multiple parts
            sparagmos
to the four directions
of the sun
gladly   to give the gift
of his heart life
of nopal fruit
of precious jade
quetzal feather
and fructifying water   (as the glyphs
to the sun   constellate
in the Smoking Mirror   the metaphor
        he was   on the painted bark paper
      the Teotl   for feathers of song
        he was   bouquet of jade flowers
to the Great Speaker   in blood speech
        he was

ensigned with mark
and color and gesture
entranced by his own song
to the priests
                    who eat the flesh
                    and the dough of amaranth
                    with their god-speech mouths
                    and wear the flayed skin
                    with skull mask of
                    Xipe Totec
                            and go dancing
                            scattering seeds
                                the cries of cut corn
                                and reed beatings
        the whistle of the eagle's claw

binding back the wheel
of time on that day
to begin again
the torn origins and the fatal order
while maidenhood
reenacts its messengers
in the married women

                               dancing once again
                               back from the milpas
                               carrying the green bud of corn
                               their hair   unbound to the wind
                               their breasts   bared to the sun
                               as if now   forever   young girls

go dancing
with cut corn
and the severed head

exchange blood
for blood
exchange heart-seed
for corn seed
feed the sun
feed the people

Out of it   they were
drunk   I think
in despotic gesture
of sacred metaphor

right in it   they were
borrachos   I think
hasta la madre de la sangre
knee deep in the gore

commerciantes crudos y sacrosantos

of the heart's men
strual blood
from what beast
of burden there was

Out of it   I think
dismembered by thought
remembered by tropic gesture
even as I am   out of it

having neither river nor stones
of this place to enliven   or bury
my mind with   their names for
my dreams' body of   blood and bones

I am no more   out of it
though unnamed   for this
coincidence of sternum
obsidian and blood green jade

All day   all night
go on   dancing
reenact   enact   and prophesy

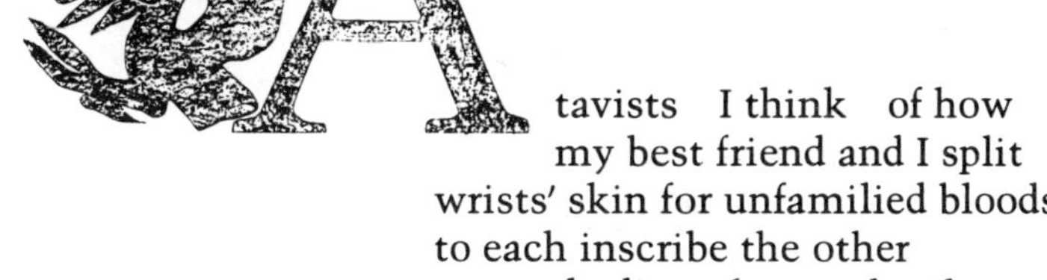

tavists   I think   of how
my best friend and I split
wrists' skin for unfamilied bloods
to each inscribe the other
on our bodies   forever brothers

yet how natural an art
ifactual   for a tribe
of two   it was to us
americus kids   all   to each
apposed to amerindian   the same

without the animate terrigenous
names   but relict of that mud   we
mimed   for our own handful of first
clay to mold   initial for bodies
uninscribed by any tracings

to mark a story for remembering
past the present two car cath
olic family   beyond which what
got chased off for   a history
wedge cut to coin a cipher

for tyrannus rex   over invest
ed to icon   an alliance divine
had   milleniums past trivia
lized the act   to this fore
closure   in what became   a child's game

as this machinery limned
to a generative logos in the stone
had taxed to death   with infinite debt
of sole origin and single treasury
the taxonomies of localized desire

inscripted with human flesh form by
reciprocal dance of feral names
to balance the differences of all
claims across hunter and animal
turfs fetished   on the body of earth

But all of that
is what we have left
to say   the didactic
to be read   nostalgic
for the song

as an exegesis of
our naivete   old chum
the forever   now unable
against the exiguous
odds   to sustain   the ode

The wish-bone   breaking
was mastadon
the blood brothers
were   aurignacian
with the same   female figurines

carved   not to cut
one image from the other
mother mammaries vulva hipped
phallic acephalous testicled breasts

but to fit   the hand for use
to count   perhaps   with dorsal cuts
the lunations for sidereal maps
to circummigrate the earth
in opposite directions

and to meet   here   again
in america   almost
total strangers at
the blind end of
the long thaw of ice

After the fact   our blood act
was only natural   but not
vestigial   to social   I mean
a sacred   yet and still merely
mimesis   to the last

of the mohicans   picture book
enacted at   the dead   hollow tree
for an absented text   to each
other for place   there but
not in a place   not there

not as leaves   to the tree   or in
a peopled book   enfolded   a child's
game   for which   that there   apoplaced
had no further play   but as
vestigial ploy   to orate   half-cocked

boys   off to   their war's way
where the imagination   misplaced
eccentric   to matrix   was   with
magazine heroine   serving
that dread's awe   full rationed

I remember that other
foreclosure   of every
version we ever played
to the tune of the twin
heroes' great exploits
invoked among the head
high weeds of the vacant

lot   was always final
ly beyond the imagi
nation's task   of what to do
without what   after the
eventual nuptials
to the proffered
but made-up maids

Only this image remains
from those years of games
the brow clenched
around that absence

the inevitable
disappointed shrug
and then homeward
if we must

to what had been
impossible to play
            (unless there was
                summer light enough
rosy for just one more
weed-slashing war

Displaced from   condensed to
as if in   a dream   rebus
a glyph   relieving the memory
        apparition now   all
at once   as its constellation
as if the maids   and the war
became   both   actual
simultaneously

    THE BAREFOOT   the big toe
of that buck-toothed   pug-nosed
flat-chested   young tease of
a girl   arc   right up my pant
leg   like that   sitting at
the sink   the shock of our flesh

that way   something there
underneath   between
the initial   one or
two   or two by two
a third   surfacing
on its flood   something
mortal   with which to do

    MY SELF   STANDING ERECT
uniformed   blue as veins
in the brick quadrangle
        (he and I both sequestered to
          different military schools)

at duck-toed attention   .
to the world war two rifle
held out for torture
at demerit's arm's length
            (the faces of the other boys   molds
               masked against the bars and the glass
               of the surrounding six stories

Then I am   throwing down   the M1
removing the brass insignia
the cap   the sam browne belt   the blue coat
the striped pants   the white shirt   the spit shoes
the tie   until finally   wasn't I
beyond me   this nakedness   down to
striated pink sinews of flesh   rose
stretched on a white stalk of bone   and the
blood thicker than their wafer and wine

which had so enraged those
shillelagh wielding priests
and their army colonels
to order me to fold and unfold
over and over again   the red
white and blue   in the triangular form
for military funerals   to present
the casket drape   to mother   sister   wife
and in every seam-fold of that flag
as that foot-arc   unclothed us all
there was   and there was more than
just her red-lipped   white-toothed   laughing mouth

            To know then   something there   more than
            as it were   underneath
            delicacies   something mortal
            with which   the others   as oneself also
            more complexed than we had played

            But not to have known   his
            accession to this
            and to never have seen
            what   for years of scrying
            only my own   dreams

            off the opaque gloss
            of our blood friendship
            it might have meant
            that he   took what was
            my given   his younger

man's fate   to become
the silent witness
that essential third
or locus for
an enactment of

that other   two   into
the one   I epistle
this to   as you   but he
will know   as her   who
delighted us both

All these years of silence
in between   now to see
that he too   in his way
as much her's   amorist there
but for more   qualmed to say

Blood brother   as such   more
I'm sure   in lieu of war
a kind of sacrifice
for which no recompense
of value in exchange

for the loss of your syntax
or the lexical   dangling
in blood knot suspension
silence   abutment to
that other third   which wrote us

named before ever   we
wailed out to its potter's
field   treasure house of
meaning in our mothers'
tongue   salvage of words

The agon   fulcrumed there
of a formula where
inspirited logos   we
weapons eclipsed   figured
for a war   of aspirations

exhaled into us from
the unlived of their   for us
gigantic lives   diminutized
among the fashioned hearth scraps
and gadgets   of likewise fostered men

When should I   could I   date
the failure in me   in him
of that formula   if at all
if even now   of his
silence within   the weaponry
under   the cloven sign
I work   this afflatus

What turns   troped him
what versions   can I
offer   still speech   afflict
ed   to explain   his silences

The narrative would be all
ways begging all ready
its own first question
for how or why with words

For a fool's   adducement
I'm seduced   by sequence
and sit here violently
swallowing the air

like a litany of knots
for unravelling to that spot

              (what was the year   sixty-eight
                Tet offensive   Nam   notched with friends
                Martin Luther King   shot
                second Kennedy   shot
                days of rage for travesty
                convention in chicago
                black studies strike at state
                run down   we were   under
                mounted horse cops   I quit
                america   first time   sixty-eight

to arrive at that spot
where I had but to recognize

the tangle of him   emerging
in the yellowed sheets
for the first time in weeks
from the mescalito dream bed

swaying in the passageway of
the kitchen of debate
reefered on the latest
oldest   totalized gematria

he stood   as if between
a word   and its antonym
unable   to come forward
or go   any further back

then threw his body at us
for a gage   on his knees
trembling   and the awe full
whispered wail   shuddering
            up like retched air   of past
            asthmatic labored breaths

                    What   the answer

and we were stopped dead
in our words   at the ends
of his hands   palsied towards
some warm   uncloven sign

    And still no answer   for
    the riddled paradox
    of words   the speaker   and
    of deeds   the doer   a

    cross the judgement's twain
    in the meager alpha
    bet   thrown dice of
    rhetoric and money

    And no formality
    to suffice against our
    own centripetal pull
    of death   First his father

    tough old   mum's-the-word   jour
    nalist   took the words with him
    then the rupture to alliance
    rended open to question

    forever   the driver's claim
    his brother   the special force's
    ranger   a suicide under
    the six wheels of the truck

    He went off after   the truth
    discovered only words
    in that absence called death
    came back with   more silence in his mouth

And there was no gift   to give
to demand him back   outward with
no dirge   solemnly to sing
no threnodial dance to body forth

that without which   the skin
sealed in ward   what rattled yet
poltergeists decomposing
all speech   for what was
        thus   Being   unspeakable

        Where people are unbound
        by any but the iron bar
        between the body and
        the letter of the law

        the syntax is a lack
        and the bodies are blanks
        for familiar phantoms
        and the colonizing

        inscriptions of monetary
        flows   thru which nothing
        given   and nothing returned
        holds   nothing in balance

            I told you so   I said
            once   before I awoke
            from a dream of mourning
            when his mother appeared
            while I cleaned the basement

            and thru the unsettled dust
            she showed me a cartoon
            and said that's who you are
            pointing to a creature
            who was his balloon of
            words   It's called   Mr. Cock
            sy   she said   when I would
            demur   or the tongue that
            filled you up   meaning   some
            how   I knew   my mother
            but in relation to
            their real life logo
            machy   about hiding
            the pain   I was   angry
            and said   so what   mistress
            of epithets   is the name
            with which to unsorcel your son

                    Then she placed her finger
                    across her pursed lips
                    and shushing me   she flipped
                    her thumb in her mouth   and mum
                    bled   can't talk with the mouth full

A knot   tied at the back
of the brain-stemmed tongue

All these years   the question
        accrues essential weight
seductive   at the edge of
        an abyss of aphasia

For you— men who do not speak
        blood brother   beyond
even the silence of
        your father   my father
men with orders   we called it
        yet catachresis of the tract
able   to give and to take   them

I also am a man
        mired in this ordure
unable to uncover
        a proper agora
of speech   double bound   be
        fore the mirror of
representation

and from this   I   fall for
        the cup of intoxi
cations   and its crazed
        as in thermo shock
to raku pots   possibilities
        to contain still   a song

All day   all night
go on dancing
reenact   enact   and prophesy

Thru carapace of the masks
the dancers mix me to
metaphors of presence
and absence   we diverse
ly live by   or with out

The dancers converge
        the hands of young women
                the blood   of young friends

threads entwined with me   at
        the eye of what needles
                mostly   commingled as

The first utterance   is
                a gift
                        then a debt

I must answer
        and to which   yet
                another responds

                all within   me only
if all history   is

now constituted   private eye
property of archaic myth
or couched symptom
        so that debt is a death
        which grows infinite
        along the search for silk
                en threads for images
                of images   to answer
                a mask given   a mask

taken   torn away to question
my face   turning from itself
in her   to mix metaphors   if
        this swaddling unwinds
        addition upon addition
        of likenesses around
                the middened place   where
                naming has been effaced
                from the flesh of the mad

men of the earth   from the
articulately dead tablets
of the madmen of the divine
        and only the abstract
        body   of capital survives
                with its surplus   organs
                of spleen and its mad
                men of the family

        And if not   if more   what
        and how comes it   to speech
        that is acting thru us all
        imminent   to further song?

With the cuetes exfoliating one
        for each of the four hundred moon
rabbits of maguey drunkeness

I make a sanctuary
within the white silences
of these four adobe walls

In all this ceremonial clamor
I take refuge   and would refuse
the scrabbling noise of America's
crescendo into a lethal silence

Let the coffee tree beside the door
tell it to the rookery stream
Let the maguey agave
tell it to the rabbit sky

I've stubbed the same toe
dance lurching along the stones
in the moon-eyed   dog-toothed dark too
many times   quiero   just a trago for a Stupa
a Candlemas of copal   to numb the throb

But edging the bet for a debt against
this dark you could drink and drink
for what only wishes
to be lost   lest it implicate
as even these dances converge

I pass the copa and hold out against
the words giving out
in the near absence
of a tongue for old stories
to go flailing

            to go beating
            like dry reeds
            for dirgeful dancing
            in and out of time

the words and the breath
to tune them to the forked tongue
I am — Los dos voces of the text
in a silence textured around

a rondo modal to

flesh burned
by its own disclosing lamp
like the god at ease
at ease in the dark

or an animal   coiled
precisely with us
in the flesh of sight
before any ocherous

images of divine beast / are limned

and to the loverly psyche
hanging fire in the middle
of the sudden mortal task
sorting the questions   in her mass

of discreetly multiple seeds

Sparagmos   a rending
a rondo   converging
a gain of unthought
in music   foot for fleeing

The night is   transparent
the night of the poem that
is   the moon is not a rabbit
is not   this drunkenness

but only the rabbit   as numerous
as the faces in the moonlight
caught glazed in the multiple
prism of the arachnoid mask
by its singular eye

The moon is   in the heavens
The moon is   at the window
The moon is   in this room
congruent to the one
mortared by speech   con
            genitally rising
            from the dugs of the dead
            above my head   beyond the
            temple   the dipper pouring down

            In this light I   know only
            the astrology of the erotic
            is oblique   is the stolen
            sun glimpse caught in the mirror
            over the horizon that makes an edge
            where even the night   might leap
            at once   and future scried apparitions
            born of flesh   but engorged by signs

The earth is now here
but if from the heavens
nowhere   but
a patterned floater
around that sun
nowhere   but
as a fix back
between two eyeings
shifting locations
thru geography
and a speech of
the first person
singular   we
assume and deflect

a musical feeling   let it be
      as it may be   more a la
Heisenberg   looking out from
      the specimen end of the micro

scope   than the fixed harmonies
      of platonic solids   I forego
and return after   across the distance
      that is the trace they would scale

            to crystal memories

The experiment is all
                          ways disturbed

Transparent
                                in the only gnosis
I can claim
                          what esters
I am able to name
                      that might catalyze a narrative

out of this alcohol burning air
                      where speech takes flame
and lights up itself
                      against the opaque sophia
of what one loves

        Some seine of flesh
                to catch its own blood
            always   already   pouring
            thru the scale of hands

        If a musical   question
                then of feeling

        the millionth   millionth
                and yet more
            as if
        division   of some monochord
        that yet entire
                    so variously entwines
                pli selon pli
        these differences

While my hand moves   still   to fill
as a circle becomes   around
the absence left by her hand
        a rondo to be   other
wise   filled and   opened out
        is how I   fugue it

My tracery of old god speech
resuscitates something
prior to it   and flows
into caves and holes
left within it   as in
limestone dissolving under water
where   with silences   we once spoke

But in this transparent night
I know these thaumaturgic tricks

The glimpse is thru cenotes
of stagnant sexual waters
where I nightly mare walk
upon the backwash waves
above the gleam
of treasured relics
and the siren bones
of drowned maidens
honed to knives
by recurrent tides
of dreams that mock
and dissolve my location

Hear the ghosts calling
crawling out of the pools
of mescal and beer
        where the phantasmic body
        surfaces upon its own flesh

            The moment is still
            everywhere now
            out of time

                    She remains
                    where the dead cicadas
                    that had swarmed
                    and rasped the air
                    along the double seam
                    of dawn and dusk
                    covered the lawns
                    that hot summer
                    and crackled so
                    beneath our feet
                    while walking in silence
                    to a place
                    in the long grass
                    to hide and find ourselves
                    at the musky edge
                    of the law of names
                    on a dangerous horizon
                    of earth and sky
                    lying down together
                    in that sudden wetness

She remains
in the rondured moon
of pools glossing
the dirt streets

the image   after argument
petra fired in the mind's
eye   one white thigh
in the moon
light   lifted care
less of the night
gown   disclosing
what in exposing
black ovate sun
spot   in the eye
glancing   I   found
sudden
ly O
pen
pink
to the kiss
of lips
and teeth
and tongue

at the breach
in our embattled lang
uage of genealogy

She remains
on the other side
of a psilocybin tenement wall
a liminal margin for a daimon urge

where the image would conjure bliss
by dismemberment
of its iconography
for the remembrance
of their cabal
to innocence and transgression
toppling all the Herms
bounding the vicious circle
of its dialectic of taboo

She remains
the other face
of memory   some
one's mother   may
be my own   with
the anxiety
flickering and receding
along the brittle edges
of the assuasive bourgeois smile

She remains
coiled   in the dehiscence
of mother and daughter
a secret   deferral
for young girls   spoken
in the mother's french tongue
as if outside the domain
of the father's   invested name

But she remains
maiden of that made world
that spoke us

She remains
maimed   Kore of the times
we remade her   image
maiden to every ad
for seedless   fruit
of the ingenue

She remains
where we made a pact
to the half-measure
of the flesh
disavowing Hell
and the seasonal nuptials
of its retributive lord

She remains
where hell had been exported
or buried in interior hollows
for leverage against one's labor
where the once divine beast
so denied   returns their own
deracinated metaphysics as thieves
in the night's random murders

She remains
full cycle of
the cicadas later
where I had to
leave her
where we couldn't
hear the silences
for the noise

Too late to whisper
the impossible secret
                    Don't Look Back

          The images do not just remain
          but conspire us with the world

          The night's cicatrix opened
     along silken threads from the mask's eye
          and slash the sword cuts
          chrysalis and branchings
          roots go dangling in the air
               of the first utterance

and the tangled voices of the blood-matted hair
     are there to tear the veil of refuge
     for this low-rent nomadic presence
     into cut clutter of partial threads
     of sweat-shop silk and homespun

          Breasts and buttocks and hands
     Carranza's guns   nightmare knives
               a frame of eyes
          Swords of the Dancers
               that cut two ways

          Indios y Christianos
          Dollars and Centavos
          head and cut corn
     gold and cupreous colored lead
          seeds falling thru
          the untuned lyre
     scattered and gathered
          in a foreign land
          where I is enmasked
          with a monetary mark
     among the men of the ejidos

Too late
the conspiratorial voice whispers

      The woman you carried
      under the dark ribs of your back
      to cradle what was other
      prior to any speech
      has returned with her pomegranate
      to rich Dis for a season

      And the woman she carried
      surfaced on the smooth mask
      for your pregnancy of transcribed desire
      was already an ad for sheer hose
      posed with lifting leg exposed

      on the steps of a bank
      that dissembled   the Parthenon
      where you could spend
      and spend with this mark
      of the encoded teller
      the unpayable letter
      of revolving credit
      across the margin of her veil

and you will be quit
rent for a song
to transform
what long ago
came undone
between   the one
and   the two
in this locus
of threes
or is this   so
to speak   always
a schema where
all fours   get squared

The moment is still
now   even as it moves
I am   transparent and
the night moves   thru me

We change   We remain
the catabolism and anabolism
of the animal eye   caught glazed
within the garish mask
or the warped viscosity
of reflecting glass

The time is of   perspective   red   shift
ing to blue in   these events   enfolding

The crickets tell the temperature
of the still mountain air
the pitch of the music rising
and falling   thru the day's scale of heat

The river is a lullaby for sleeping
an old dream   time muttering
of rock and plant and water magic
beside   the bougainvillea window
a constant narrative
that flows where it may
at once   its mountain provenance
and its destiny of the sea

The waterfall is more erratic
with leaping from crag to rock
and yet it remains the same
cataracting out of its own archaic cut
thru the layers of earth-heaved stone
beside the steep temple stairs

The women   who daily unravel
their bundles of linen to wash
along the river's rock banked pools
send the young ones off
to the old one   the water
fall   the story
teller   to unravel and explain
the bad drunks and the ecstasies
of their fathers and the pulque god
who   after conquest   was a
bottom less cup   which remained

Bucket by bucket
day by day
this is how   I steal

or invent   this place
drawing my wash water
like a mirror of quicksilver

in my hand   back
away   from the looks
and the laughing   women

censured of   singular eyes
for a young man   alone
with his shirts   and his sheets

Draft by draft
one narrative stops
and another begins

the voices are caught in the bucket
the air is clear and pollened
thick with warm sunlight

The masks appear and disappear
in the whirlpool closures of time
catching twigs in the river's weirs

The face comes back
in the tangible bucket
with the algae

and the seeds of wildflowers
and the volcanic silt
sifting thru the wider eye

reading the feeding
and fucking habits
of the mercurial spiny fish

that leaps the banks
to find the stream
in an other narrative

that calls soundlessly
to its double
enfolded by the same

In such silences as these
  my voice is of the cicadas
returning out of time into its song

But while we were coming undone
one had nothing to say
other than the friction of frail wings
and that chafed fledgling was but
one wing addressing the other
stiffened in time to a silence
without further communion

Where it left us   that in
nocence before speech
so interfaced with our speech
unable then to speak
our own words   or act
for our place in that place

Where I left her
among voices bartering
that arduous sanctity
of speech
for more and more
of the less and less
coincident to a real world

among the flesh not whole
cloth worn but hung
from the greedy bone
stumping to the end
less labor of no
love   to limbs loosen   comes

among the mumblings in high places
among the gun-grumblings in subways

among the howling
to be heard   unheard
by the deadened ears

among the posturing frenzy
to be seen   unseen
in the whites of their eyes

among the faces
maimed to a mask
of diminishment

among what she
could so easily
call home   Oh
protect her
whatever to blame

Finally   hang the sweet
innocence with the other
phantoms from the greased
gantries of the times

Finally   my own failure
at what I couldn't tell her
from the manchild lover's first mask

            roiled as I was   in my own
            obscurities for a language
            of stars and the hiero
            glyphs of the dead   magicians
            to catch and call and lose the love
            in Pythagorean crystals of the poem

that even our bed had been
colonized by masked bandits

Sweet bed   lovers still   I
was the barbarian of the Republic
with sweet lies of muthos in the mouth
of metonymy   to all else   we
missed in the land of plenty
she kissed   while we were counting

the dreadful corpses

      the burning monks

         and the dandy daddies

of the front line news

that phantomed   by tracer
bullets on the surface
of our bedroom flesh
the body of insatiable sacrifice
we were inhabited by
to scapegoat an entire nation
for the shibboleth of a name

        Dirty Commie   so obscured
in what got bought and sold
that even in protest   we
could not see the immanence
of death's residency

        while she read Celine
and Cosmopolitan Magazine
and insinuated novels
for the manhood of fame
and fortune against the war

        And I talked and wrote
and walked and signed with
the righteous in the white light
of day   and drank booze to
a bullying rage at her   behind
the bed and door at night

Oh   Protect her
where she lies
down in that
slime so clean

        Finally   one had nothing to say

        but in such silences as these
            with the noise of the cuetes
            again echoing the voice
            of the drunken god up
            from the earth of men and women
            barbaric enough
            for this place and time
            to be so playful with their awe

        my voice   like the cicadas
        like the cuetes for
        a rabbit in the moon
        abides its own echoing song

Though if ever we are a tune
to ourselves   the time is off
among partial tones   unheard
in the dominant   we strike

          There is this   dissonance
          between speech and acts
          We can't get back   on the tonic
          home now is   always   a new place

Thus this pre tense to dance   on   from
between the dissonance   its beat
when the legs are nearly foundered
by cherished stones in the pockets

          So why glance back
          to reopen this gap
          for the chorus
          with the blood-matted hair

Except like the river
          as the song sings   out of
phase   its signs   to flow with
          where the lay of the land
lies   estuarial   there where the body's tied

Except being   so out of time
          the sign   assigns her face
among the masked dancers
          her hands in the light
ciphered touch of the crowd

renders the circle of
this other body   text
ured to repeat   Dissonant

demands that one song to rend
between the boy and the man
what   if not sung into this

one oddly congruent night
might   need again   be desire
's difference   resurfaced

for the light of day   in the dark
ly apparent   transparent   paean
to death   like avowing for a mask
at the mouth gagged with signs

against the life which might be
nightly   by night ulceration
memory   thru seine and sieve of
this other moon's peptic tides

Except   in consort to
this dissonance   to expect
for further song   after this
first utterance
demands the helping hands
        of likeness   to follow the lost
                thread   in difference
                    home to
                            metonymy

for all else   we missed
                            postulate with
the pellicular
the axiomatic
                            edge of this
            chiasmatic kiss

First   the mask   to find
this place   with her face
for my face I   can't find   if
it   only undressing my camouflage
    like a chameleon on a mirror
            hoping to hide   is
                in a uni verse
                        of it self

where the repeated   only
pattern of colors   remains
as even   the light curved
                            back on itself
in the mirror of our eyes

Except to remember

"Each loses what he chooses"
"he said" "as I   said" in
side   what "as I am   always
talking" "thinking" it   is "mine" or
a "choice"   as it might   "simply" be
"I will" "as mind   is a finger
pointing" "wonder" as   far as that
"wisdom"   goes   into what is

"a place to be"   beyond the
choosing   if such so   some other
dream enfolding   this one
or that one   or this one
with the silence of the rocks
and the real roses and the
yellow alacrán under
the red pallet   and the distant
touch even of this weather

which also   seem to choose
though more   "simply"   than   "I"
mean   are there   and do move
"use"   by that which is not
identical to   but is   it
self   not opposed each to
each   but enfolded by same

Accept this
to remember   by
as I wander periplum home
towards this enfoldment
for a place   that I
said No to the Not
inherent in my own
was it   proposal   for a
marriage to consum
mate the inherited
signs   for a choosing
against losing the
assumed identities
in the already sub
sumed genealogies

                    I was the juvenile
                    one   they would say
                    in the remnant families
                    but it was two or three
                    or four   all together
                    more   voices than just
                    delinquent intonation
                    for the drone song   upon
                    the face of it   a fascicle
                    unbounded by any
                    single decipher
                    ment to fashion
                    their exoskeleton
                    for a viable mask

Was it
was this how
"love" foundlinged us
                              (at sixteen   Oh way before
the whole of what light
fell upon   opened end in
the eye   arc   lit swarms first in
the caverns of the selfs   textures
actually   across   it's edge
was sexually enticing   form
          was nomadic flow and
                    thought   was dissemi
                         nation   vitrified

to survive the catoptric
struggle for a singular
fiction in the face
to emit and decipher
the coveted signs   thru which

          a kiss is not a kiss
                    a smile is not a smile
                         a teat is not a teat

as we are   marked with no
tation to the dis

appearance of the body
fleshed   prerequisite to

its appearance as sign
whose meaning is desire

whose body is demand
its presence   to be ensigned

for simultaneous proof and den
ial   the exclusive   shrine   of "love"

This difference between
motors the great machine
of our cloven inhabitation

By fits and starts
its perpetual motion
moves eden to Ur staat
in the regime   of desire

is desire of desire
harnessed to   the massive wheel
producing widgets and cogs

in the play of signs
to displace the cloven hoof
sublate the multiplicity
of earthly and celestial signs

multiply the surplus value
of the abyss between
the sign for a proof of "love"
and the milk of the body of flesh

sell it short   into the only
market there is   the coffers
of the few   and we are
condensed to heads or tails
of a coin whose images
conspire us with its world

where our desire is
    inhabited to be
            the great fascist
            behind the latest
            lawnmowing machine

where our desire is
    inhabited to be
            the suicided sex queen
            cooking the latest milk
            cheese and meat substitutes
            in the carcinogenic tupperware

Accept it
perhaps   to say
it has always been
bitter to come of age
since what literal time
it was   that meant
the loss of the world
and not its gain

Except it   to remember
the time is   always off
andante   skipping live
ly across   the gap of self
reflection   to abridge   the some
how harmonic   tempo of difference

To remember   I said   I'm older
than that   She said   younger
you mean   Hunter   I said

I remember   I said   I'm going
hunting   I'm going running
scared   so hungry for a song

I'm going hunting   for a song
I'm going hunting   for a face
thru which   so unseen   to disappear

as if thus to lose not just
the impoverished reflection
in the coin of the realm   but
the silver nitrate of the mind

And then the unforseen
trying to pass   dressed
to the part   dark   with mustache
how fast   it comes   bursting

back to awe   the full song
from the multiple pores of the face
the space between   this text
ures the undifferentiated

mass   Her hands within
the swarm of cicadas   and
cicada killer wasps
upon the cymbaled ear

reinstates the herm
eneutics   of one's own
ly being   here   other
while   thusly ensigned

I remember   I said
    No   again   on the highway
            I remember
I said   Go Hunting then
when the man at the dusty puesto
laughed   pointing at the indians
leaving the main highway
and said   They're going hunting

I said   Go Hunting
        it will be remembered
                with eyes open
                        to every direction   Go
                        Hunting for Elder Brother
                        Deer   Wawatsari

                        Taste the sweet venison
                        it is the flesh
                        of the skeleton soul
                        of the alert hunter

                        nibble at the leaves
                        like the Elder Brother
                        and he will come to you

Go Hunting   Wawatsari
go with the short bow
beating the song
of Mara akame
the master of fire
who leads you home
with power woven in his hat

Leave the face for the village
in the village
Leave the milpa
Leave the wife
Leave the husband
Leave your given name
It will be remembered

Take up your new name
for the journey   recite
the story for each and every
lover   before all the people
before grandfather   fire
tie   the sisal knots for
each name   each kiss   each
caress   and genital exposed
to the fire as you dance

with laughter of acceptance
throw the knotted sisal into
the mind of fire   Tatewari
be born again   before the desire
of your sex   take up now
your new name   and promise
to tell all   all you find
to find our lives
It will be remembered

Go with the sacred arrow
to pierce the life heart
of Wawatsari in the green
suckling flower of peyote
in the desert north
of San Luis Potosi

Walk to the mountains
of the mothers and fathers
Go Hunting
Elder Brother Deer
in Wirikuta
It will be remembered

I remember
as the procession of Huicholes
left the main highway
for the geography of dream
which is their ancient home
Wirikuta   of no literal
                inhabitation   they gathered
                all the dead branches
                to transform by fire
                the bones of Elder Brother Deer
                for his vision   they will be
                come   in his light   his flesh
                in mortals of a transparent world
                for their skeleton souls
                in their flesh dream
                vision they will be as one
                that many-textured form

                metonymy
                to all else
For what we missed
I sang for them
as if it had been my song

I sang for them
with my going
with their words
remembered from books

remembered out of other
meanings   enfolded by the same
for peyote transformed Boston

Remembered out of my hunger
as the man laughed
saying   they're going hunting

Go hunting   I whispered
It will be remembered

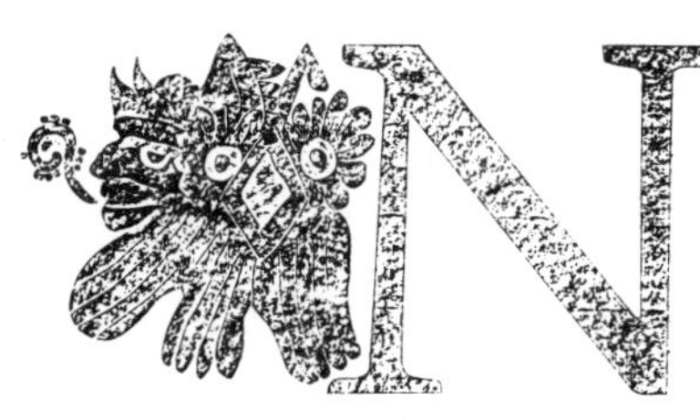

ot my song
            not my mountain
not my mother
        nor my father
not my Wirikuta
        nor my naming
not my home
        in metaphor

But it is remembered
        without the metonymic
        emblems of any tribe

Remembered
            thru the rhythm as
        once perhaps genealogy was
        strung to as pearls of
        names for animals plants and men
        this rhythm now confounds
        the category shot back thru
        its own representation
        al space to waves of fib
        rillation in the same song

The divergent dances
                              converge in this song
              across the deferance
                              of the distances
              across the difference
                              of the codes
              even as the rondo goes
                              open
                    undone in a ravel of
                              odds

This song   the very seam
                              of difference
a sortilege of threads
                              enfolded by the same
unscalable in any one mode
                              either to the depths
of cellular fossils
                              or the surface
of the sexual phantoms
                              in the flesh

              not the body socially inscribed
              not the body divinely symbolized
              not the body numbered to the coin
                              of any equivalency of exchange
not caught in any recourse
                              to a name

The same song   say

where the linear discrete polypeptide chain of co
         valent Identity-bonded Amino Acids
              are questions of difference
                 for their own answers
              the neighborhood provides
                 as the chain folds
                    spontaneously
                    to the tune of
                    more than self
                    description
                    in the omni-
                    directional
                    enzyme bonds
                       for a 3-D
         catalytic machine
                              to tap out the time
              for the syncopation
                              of the tune

The same song   say
where the concatenated
seeds for a narrative
are burst open   with ergot alkaloids
              and the webs of tracery
         disentangle the dearest phantoms
              from saint's and sinner's
                 catatonic theater
          of deaths and other temptations
      thru transparent vibratory palimpsests

where the eye surfaces the flesh
upon a world that mirrors back
liquid-eyed world to disclose
beneath the phosphorescence
the stutter   at the edge   of the flesh
the struggle   with his sudden fallen angel
of indication   whose most ancient
algebra   finger pointing
              is severance
                          of mutual negation
by which the world
                          is   and is not itself
sees and eludes itself

              Where the narrator is
              sentenced to time
              until he is its song
              in the folding of
              his cloven angel paradox
              thru which he reenters himself
              before his speech
              can inscribe
              a serpent
              swallow
                          ing
                             its tail

he same song
        remembered

Where the eyes were seer as seen
where the flesh was toucher as touched

thru which we were knocked
from our single pivot
for a known world
        as if dropped
                back thru
our own representational
space   falling thru   our events
in retrograde and sideways   the net
they made of us   unraveling
to the unthought   of catch and seine

as each and every of the all
inclusive   house on a hill
above city horizon   window
wall   tapestry of rain   the
thousand eyes on the bodies
of lover and friends   a
swim in arabesque of lace
— burned up or was
melted or was other
wisely transformed
and informed itself none
the less   as all
the rest   the flesh was
all burning branches
blue hot in the heat
of our bellowed furnace flame
feeding light to forgotten sites
left darkly carbonized
by the hierarchic brain

      the moment standing still
          in such immeasurable motion
      the night dense and transparent
          in such pellucid light

as we   as the mind   melted
as the flesh flowed
one into the other
without the boundaries
of any formerly classified
erotic   the naming marks
like a Not   if left locked in
to itself   of the skin

                    (so that later   venturing
                    the berserk city streets
                    we saw as one beast
                    the snarling white man
                    chasing the bleeding black man
                    out the scream echoing cafe door
                    with the long silver-red carving knife

saw this as one
self-severed beast
of its own suicide
seeing as we had just begun
seeing   the long swelling
of ourselves thru earth flesh
and not just the moment's spume
that mote by motive caught the eye
and at a loss convinced the flesh
its sex   its delicate pellicle of skin
was abrasion   was only itch and scratch
of an erithism that could tickle you
could torture you   one against
the other   down to death

But I lose the thread
        that was later   after
        not another story
        but a different thread
        that descends
        into the city's hell
        where we came down
        as they say
        against the ground
        upon which we must also
        figure
                        the meaning
        I mean
                        the context
        for survival
                of our embrace

But it is the embrace
I am speaking of
the song I was thinking of
where we were disclosed
in the unsuspected   giddy laughter
at the loss of our own
bodies' tortuous   tickling edge

When I couldn't know
                if my hand
was between your thighs
                or mine
or if it was your hand
                or mine
or if the other   yours
                or mine
was in your mouth
                or mine
                    or some other
                        soft   wet   circle
                of muscles
or whose tongue it was
                where
                    I couldn't know
to speak with
                all to say
                    in the mouth   I
couldn't call my own
                was all there   was
for the gain
                of such loss
to say
                echoing laughter

where time   loses   its motion
to mass   and mass   is no thing
but motion   within   and without
specific   destination   inter
relating   by phases   of heat
call it bliss   if you will   or music
informing   photons to   constellations

and this awakening
                              and falling asleep
             was the body's long dream
the long swell   beneath the spume
           that awakens our bodies
           to magma and mammal tides
              we crest on
           in our chanced sharing
               of blood pulsing
             thru coacervate eyes
               casting light
               and shadow
         on the intaglio cracked walls

            light and shadow
            casting form
            in footprints
            of ancestral feet   I
            follow   we   we
            all the way home

he wall is no wall
  but the pellucid
membrane of the eye   we
see thru the same viscosity
we share the self-same vision
at the edge of our skin   we
freely move out and in luck
to be   so fluidly
in ease of early love
permeable and uncontained
The wall is no wall

The wall is whirling agate
the wall is petrified wood
the wall is tapestry of rain
swaying with the wind

The wall is lattice of
the loins oscillating thru
the eyes and skin   the wall
is uterine membrane of night
time sky in the window

blue canals of moon
red veins of Mars   the wall
is amniotic water   meaning
drops thru the transparency of
with the selfless attention to
those bright pebbles skipped
in that black-blue upside down pool

The ripples spread eccentrically
crossing senses and sensibility
approximating multi-centers
at the abandon of all measures

     Star Nebulae   and   Skeleton Radiolaria
          Star Coral   and   Spiral Algae
               Absolute symmetry of Volvox
               in a downpour of shooting stars

curled tortion of protein
          effloresence of rain forests
               nets of neural axons
                    wind over water
                         red lava thru black rock
the hide on a zebra's back

Blue copper jellyfish
          seducing the genitals off
               every shadow's sex
                    in a pool of water and oil

Iguanas of jade silver opalescence
          opening the imbricated
               spore dropping ferns

Gold viruses turning crystal
          geometries thru topologies
               of cellular mitochondria

Racoons caught
          in garbage cans
The faces in subway windows
          the hands and eyes and mouths
               of lovers and friends

Rose sturgeon leaping
in the flesh we are
the splash of   in the
cross-rippled footprints
of falling spores
along the neural ridge
of the wall

where light and shadow
is the first distinction
for the liquid eye
to inform lacework image
towards a pulsing script
manifesting itself there

Quanta   now in shadow   Wave
wall as carboniferous dark
implodes the flesh to light
in a drool of diamonds

Quanta   now in light   Wave
wall as vertebrae
skull and ribs

Quanta   now in shadow   Wave
wall as boulevard
of an ancient city

Quanta   now in light   Wave
wall as crystal
of earth metal

Quanta   now in shadow   Wave
wall as meadow
of grain grasses

Quanta   now in light   Wave
wall as corn sheaf
flows in
to the snout
of the snail

Quanta   now in shadow   Wave
                        wall as galaxy trail
          of the snail flows in
                       to the teeth of the dog

Quanta   now in light   Wave
                        wall as the dog
       tooth star flows in
                       to a circle of fire

Quanta   now in shadow   Wave
                        wall as flames
               flow in
                       to the uterine mouths
       of song-filled friends

Quanta   now in light   Wave
                        wall as eyes
            of friends
                 flow in
     to the curl of worms

Quanta   now in shadow   Wave
                        wall as worms
               flow in
                       to the tangle of roots

Quanta   now in light   Wave
                        wall as darkness
             flows in
                       to flower

Quanta   now in shadow   Wave
                        wall as bright seeds
               flow in
                       to the beaks of birds

                    that lift
                on ravels of wind
            between the charred stars
            and the arrival of their light
    out of shadow   on the light

                beating their wings
irredescent   with eyes on

                the goat drum skin

                    of me

            suddenly sinew stretched
            and flexed by heat of hand
        between thew and softer thigh
    mixing webs of   pungent music
    with this ambrosia   of ammonia

                    piss
                    fish
                    fecal
                    roe
                    sexual
                    seep
                    and
                    sweet
                    salt
                    sweat
                to attune me
            with the perfect
            pitch of you

    From this lambent light that for its passage
            upon no medium depends
            we are drawn down in
            to dense writing

                darkness

            where music rises up
        measuring what vibrates
        where the matter is
        most what matters
        meaning measured so
        the dancer is the music
        the music is the dance

The drum holds the music   the silences between
      hold the rhythm of the heat from the heart
              drum to the head and the hand

                    purling

        our scents that hold us and our laughter
          that lets us loose into a trembling
                  like mitosis

                    cutting

        the encradling   threads of light
        into the double   unbinding of our joke
    surprised enrapturing   to be already moving
        after these airs   of distinct musks
          that rive and   and signal that
            which mingles us most

                No thot   but that
                  Thou art that
              where no platonic names
              lay claim harmony's scale
                only parameters
                like our bodies
                in form the music
                of this swarm
                ing multitudes
        of no "mommy" or "daddy" born

FIGURE   AND GROUND
oscillates   you and me
we dance   from foot
to foot   to figure
the tempos   for equivalencies
that arise   and recede
in harmony   of choral song
we are a balance   in body gesture
quick leaping   over sloughs
of thought's   sluggish rests
the rhythm is   the melody
as flesh   its song

sounding

thru shuttling threads
of muscles and light
unsquarable
warp and woof
coiled and layered
arteries and veins
the blue articulates the red
the black articulates the light
we come back to   the same gesture
as if in the palms   of a gesture of prayer

WINGS OF CICADA

we open are opened   the flesh by flesh upon
we coil are coiled   with the world of the flesh
we merge   into depth
out of depth   we emerge
out of larvae   at the root meaning
spirit or mask   we are disclosed
out of the cave   of shadow plays
wings of spume   nymphae   dehiscing   for swelling wave
out of pupae   twined lips   of the flesh   a babe of each sex
touching   so   touchable
kiss
major mode to   labia   minor descant
white thighs diverge   black ovate eye

opens
lungs
and
mouth
with
seeds
under the tongue

WINGS OF CICADA
in the cells of the body
converging chiasma
across sweet sacrifice
offerings
of the boundaries
where we might bleed

calling up blood to be earth
hard but so tractable
as so soft where I touch you
giving us birth
in and out
we go
to intertwining so
that rising up as we
on this the first day
do in the darkly joining
there is no reflected shock
of absence to assuage
this firmament does not divide the waters from the waters

ut with deference
            by light and shadow
casting in form
        from a candle
burning up from
        both ends—blue black
waxed wick and gold
        glowing air—I bit

the soft spot between
        Mons Venus
and pelvic bone
        for a mark of difference
from which to move
        with the face of passion
arisen up out of depth
        over the surface
of the once familiar face

I felt no pain
        and your hips twisted
it all with pleasure
        to a question
whose answer was
        more of the same

There was no pain
        though the mark was there
where we each suddenly appeared
        My teeth were of a language
that your hips spoke as a song
        calling them up to the tune
from the mute hunger
        that gnawed at a world

of both out and in
        giving birth between
birth and this siren song
        to the shadowed daimon urge
and the hidden teeth of the gods
        to heaven and hell
and the whole contested cosmos
        hanging from the sign of our teeth

calling us up with a vengeance
        for the beauty of presence
caught so panicked with the nakedness
        of its pumping predicament
sucking and thrusting thru
        an infinite regress
at the clonic oozing fold
        of ass and thighs
that the I had been consumed
        that the one in the mirror
was just smoke
                from smouldering ash
        of this inherited mask
                the burning body unmakes
        when it finally awakes

In the cleft of that moment
there was no other but mute
speech for the quick glimpse:
each body was its own face

        and the heart seemed to stop there
        in the middle of the dance
        as if released from the trance
        of its own swinging rhythm

and then it started again
swinging us between
branches of artery and vein
between sleeping and waking

        between hunger and satiety
        between pleasure and pain
        and at the fictive middle of its arc
        we spoke each other's given name

This bliss   escapes us now
          thru the seal of the grave
n letter   the graven
image that seals   our pleasure
with the solace of the law
for the deferral of the dead
we reincarnate   to reinvent
a veil of sleep
for the syncope of the day

Let it   it is congruent also
to this night that desires it
to this moon we say mirrors it
to this poem that can speak
only of its own events
even as it would disentangle
this doubling of its first utterance
to actually dance you to its tune

Let it   and call it
as this coin falls
our ritual   so we may know
what yet costumes the skin
          with the unsuspected graph
          of trace threads from a childhood's air
          we breathed   a metaphysics
          of our mother tongue
          that returns to us
          an icon of all loss

"Alas, for flowery, mushy, sappy twenty
and the sharp persian sword . . ."

Let it   worry memory's beads
with the mortmain of paradigm
for the distraction
                of the pettifogger
                the petty bourgeois
                and the political ideologue
who bequeath me this failing
for representation of the flesh
for this transcription of desire
to desire not death
but what is already perfectly dead
Naturaleza Muerta   they call
these images in museums here
or still lifes   we call them

                where language is
                        as person becomes
a commodity   of waged labor / or owned decor
                        a simulacra
                                of the significant despot
                                or the fetish of the fruitful earth
                        a weapon
as invisible as
cyanide in the air
tuned to the private familiar scale
for public-private capital gains

where the woman
                all but
lacks the lineaments
of the desire denied
to this speech
and yet remains
                the fetish
        conspiring us with the world
                still cherished
in the body of the text
to leaven the question
of love and submission
                        (the world made safe
                                for love and democracy
                        insphinxed by complicity
                                to this representational pleasure
                        once so dismantled
                                by a dangerous bliss

So the pain is a grinding
along the margins of what
turns on itself
is torn from itself
at the rents of paradox
where it reenters itself
but seems not to move

a rondo   a fugue
a whetstone of contradiction
sharpening the poem's lapidary tools
to inexorable knives
with double edged blades
which can not but excise
both virulence and bliss

Where your flesh was
                with mine
but now escapes
                from just that place
                in the epistle
where your name is
annealing to significant stone

Yet of course I miss
finding the true mark
with this alphabet of blades
I cut every where
and nowhere at once

I cut the ground out
from beneath me in
an empyrean quest

The truth is a draft of hemlock
we drink to suicide the unique
into the rhetoric of the day

The truth is a tooth
of speech   let's say
used to bite and seduce some
body's mother body   may
be you   or me
put it under the pillow
of our dreams
for a coin with two faces
inscribed with two images
equal to only one value
            can you follow the thread
of power   by complimentary threat
to each in our privatized flesh
where the truth precipitates
immunity to the question
receding with the limits of
a mortgage on the father's name

The truth is   let's say
toilet training
given speech and a law degree
to cantilever against
the wind and the rain

The truth is as
the language goes
always already trop
ic   crystalization of
old metaphors   he said
turning crystals   like
he said   tumblers of
locks thru the light
a gain like snow
flakes that can melt
in the bliss of a moment's
            hot hand

The truth is   always
already elsewhere
in the question   of signs
different from that which
meaning   with no in
duced   deduced or
seduced single pivot
less simply   just is

The truth is   that
which could never
quite be said
not even too late
of what we felt

                    (though I choose to speak
                        and accept the mask
                            of the monkey for it

                    Thoth   to fashion our babel
                        in closing circles
                            precedent to opening

                    the body into silence

                    even as I chose you to unmask
                        to precipitate the sexual to masks
                            out of the obscure mirrors

                    and shadows of our families
                        for the unraveling of
                            a prophetess' sooth

                    to our little mummer's great
                        mother's riddle for the dis
                            appearance of Imago Mundi

For what we felt
and had no image
nor need to name
to include ourselves in

the Numinous   a dated
phrase   to prop against
the jargons of the age
that make a horror
out of   as the fictions
in the speech are
disclosing   Nothing

else to turn to
or ascend thru
but this place
of birth and death
nowhere   but a fix
backwards and forwards
between the eyes
in any two heads
that fixing cannot see

The Numinous is not
bounded by the lover's
bed   nor do its ways
enclose on such singular stages
though we may enact all
the contests of
the made world there
with imagined mark and gesture
of an old uprooted sacred

Finally to say   just
that   seems so clear   after
travelling   so far   thru
speech and geography
to arrive at a place
where I could say   just that

as if   once given the mask
of a power to wear
in the enactment of a season
I could see from inside
its enlarged eyes what was denied
by our daily   frightened purpose

and could feel   some great heart
swinging back and forth
thru months of too much rain
and months of no rain at all
and know no more   than that

Let this replace
the deferment of my speech
so that I may be given this place
to withdraw the defense from
its theatre of accusation

Let's both hang
this image
of the sweet innocence
from the greased gantries
of the times   cantilevered
against the wind and the rain

I can't go back
more than this
and you can't but remain

In the skip of a heartbeat
is the failure of an age
we couldn't see come of age
until we could suddenly see
        thru this hiatus of the heart
                daily filled by the bullroaring
                magic rhombus of machines
        what was taking so long
                in its dying
                    all that remained
                        only person and property
to be absolutes
                    for a judicial theater
of the Res Publica

But oh   we thought
we were too young then
to be so possessed
by either absolute fiction

as we were still listening
to the faint voices
of the old gods
awisphering
thru the kingdoms
of the families

and we were listing
to the more insisting
gods of no territories
amurmuring
thru the flesh

We lived between
the seams of these two worlds
as we sought   first
by innocence   and then
by transgression   our own
theater   for a third world
to detain the portent of both

By advance and retreat
of these liminal tides
                drawn towards neap-tide
                by quadrature
                of the specie's
                        all powerful eye
                and the angled moon mirror
                                (filtering beauty in the light
                                        of our eyes by a chemistry
                                        of altering desire

we appeared and disappeared
from our own gaze into
the well of the body's desire
                wishing with gamblers' coins
                minted out of first flames
                of capillary heat
                for an image to arise
                        (as if naturalized for heliotropes

                                as sugar and root water
                                drawn thru stem to sun
                                is crystalized to the net
                                of its own ripening fruit

We were such sweet barter to each
in sexual speculation
between the faceless image
of the dream and the looking
glass mask of the lover

What was invested within us
so doubled between us
to break open the rondo of our dreams
for a secret light in the other's eyes
and then to image its shadow play
for the politics of a pleasure
as representative of the same

so that from the unnamable
of our secret we formed
a substance for ourselves
by trading what was
as if maimed in one
for what was hale if not
whole in the other to
a construct of each
incorporated for effigy
and disposed to
a shorthand of history

as if   let's say
a romance   with song
and dance   about
the developing stages of capital

Sweat-shop laundry owner's daughter
marries corporate Comptroller's son

                              in the end

we couldn't both be
traitors   so we traded

That beautiful mouth
for the hazel green eyes

the crooked legs
for the crooked nose

the delicate baby hands
for the cleft in the chin

the odd black hairs
between the breasts
for the blotchy adolescent skin

the aquiline algerian nose
for the tiny wrist bones

the gracious   nervous laugh
for the serious mustache

the french mother's tongue
for the occasional poem

the devoted   daughterly family
for the dangerous   crossroads sons

the class valedictorian
for the dreamer in truancy

the mask of the virgin
for the mask of the satyr

the art of good manners
for the clowning rage of bad drunks

the afternoons of tea and tennis
for the nights of wrecked cars

the junior league balls
for the run-ins with the law

the strictly soda-pop suburban princess
for the jazzed   nickel-bagged   Kubla Khan

the one at home   there
in the assumptions of love
for the one at home nowhere
but in the exceptions of love

But that's not it
not our secret   but some half
life   calculus for the parts
of our fascination with
the image of the other
that we traded for
a talisman to our sex

Fascinus   the deed or act
Fascinus   the roman amulet
of the phallus   we bartered for

presence and absence
puppeting the flesh
warring at the digit
al boundaries of this
desire   to be and not
to be   subject of
        object of   and
        cause of   all
at once   for an
eternalization of
this desire in   and there
for and by   the sarcaphagic sign

Fascinum   the evil eye

to be bewtiched and be warlocked
by a dangling modifier
and an erected metaphor
in the imaginary discourse
                between the amulet and the act
                between the family and the desire
                between the body of capital and
                        the labor of love

                You were the answer
                I was the question

                I was the answer
                you were the question

                The world doubled
                and doubled again
                until the secret
                was a square root
                for the algorithm
                of the invisible hand
                in commodity exchange

                until its law was a wall
                where we were dismembered
                on the cutting edge
                between what remembers us
                and what we remembered
                ourselves by

until the wall dissolved
and we reentered the flesh
that remembered us
by dismemberment
of dismemberment
that night in Boston
when we forgot how
to remember ourselves
in what we were
remembered by

and I couldn't go back
there was no traitor to that

If you had asked me then
did I love you
I could only have lied
or uttered an inarticulate cry

I loved you then
as I loved myself
in such bliss

with perfect selfishness
a kind of selflessness
not presuming to be
any I am who am

but being   just the same
as you   for me   for you
not quite   myself

but a world
you take   as
I take it
we make it

But I must tell you now
with the dancers still dancing
in the extended night of the poem
and the mescal of the pulque
god on my mind for the heat
of this long   mercurial song

It seems from here
that there is no set
in any calculus
of love or sex
or this rare mathematics
of speech   breaking open
its rondo to song
that has itself as a member

        except as the I of this poem
        or the eye in the ritual mask
        interfaced immediately
        with the paradox of its double
        enactment for the gift
        of meaning   as one voice woven
        from multiple cavernous songs
        polyphonic to the choral world

As the heart goes swinging into song
between strophe and anti-strophe

it reenters itself   a klein form
thru topologies of no literal statement

that might   as you   otherwise   desired
reassure one   to be one   and to remain

one   like a title before a name
or a life   insurance policy claim

I peer out at firelight
rippling on the surface of water
that spreads in tributaries
of what we are
remembered thru   now
only the pattern remains

the water of the river
enmeshed with the light
makes it visible to me

as the love remains
enmeshed with the voices
echoing out of time
to remind me
that the light curls
back on itself
in no one's eyes

And in such transparency as this
I flinch back from this retribution
of having the last word from
my house   mortared   and raised
lazaro like   by speech

against your inhabitation
in the image   of some other
less severe   less awful
less disonantly musical
perhaps   less marvelous   world

And I am remembered   in
the love you were   womanly
perhaps   better able   to retain
in that so diminished
night light of our secret
in which I could   no longer remain

This too is our gage
for the nothing   now
recirculated thru
its own differences   that I
had also invested
against the severance
of what I had then to say

But even in such obscurity
as I force it against the grain
of the poem   I do choose
again as I let loose
to the tributaries
of this water that will return
thru othered words
as blood to the body of the poem
in the circulation of signs
the image of the other and the
squint-eyed masks we made and gave

In its place the poem claims
for my monkey nakedness
a mask   once of this old place
of half-skull   half-flesh
painted with a garish smile

I do choose
before it's all a dune
of sand and the dust
of human and animal bones
to hold as sacred
this most swinging
                        (like the heart
mask that enlivens me
with how things may live
and how things may die
that we might enact it
and ourselves again
in chorus with the actual

swinging against
    the eternalized   mortified
    of desire's desirous trace
    in the regime of the logos

swinging against
    death's immanence
    in the regime of silence
    by which thanatos   is
    the only prophecy

        With this mask
        I do choose
        to go hunting
        with eyes open
        to every direction

        With this mask
        I do choose
        to go on dancing
        and with 'the stones
        in my pockets

All day   All night

to reenact

          enact

             and prophesy

NOTES

BIRD GLYPHS used in the design of the capital letters are one series of such images which represented the count of one thru thirteen for the Aztecs. The sacred calendar, the tonalpohualli, which counted the two hundred and sixty day ritual year, consisted of twenty periods of thirteen days. There were twenty day names—such as calli (house), coatl (snake), malinalli (grass), tochtli (rabbit), etc.—which combined with the numbers, one thru thirteen, designated the day count, such as 1-grass, 2-reed, 3-ocelot, etc. to 13-lizard. At the end of the thirteen count the next period began with the glyph of the number one coupled now with the glyph of the day which was second in the previous series. Thus the calendar may be imagined as two circular gears, one with cogs of the glyphs of the thirteen numbers, and one with the cogs of the glyphs of the twenty days, which slip ahead one cog for each full turn of the wheel of thirteen. In this way, when the wheel of twenty has made one full circle the ritual year is complete. Following the formality of this image of the eternal return evolving, the first glyph in the poem is repeated again in what would be the fourteenth position in an ordinal count.

The glyphs appear in Seler, Eduard; "Das Tonalmatl der Alten Mexikaner", *Gesammelte Abhandlungen Zur Amerikanischen Sprach–Und Allertermskunde*, Vol. 1, Graz, Austria, 1960.

PULQUE, (American Spanish) of obscure etymological origin; post-Cortesian name for Nahuatl, Octli, the intoxicant of the peoples of the valley of Mexico; fermented from the sap of the maguey plant, a member of the Agave family, from whence the present day tequila is a distilled refinement.

Vide: Goncalves de Lima, Oswaldo, *El Maguey y el pulque en los Codices Mexicanos*, Fondo de Cultura Economico, Mexico, 1956 and Seler, Eduard, op. cit. Vol. 2, "Die Tempelpyramide Von Tepoztlan" pp. 200-214; and "Das Pulquefass der Bilimek'schen Sammlung", pp. 913-952.

CARRANZA, VENUSTIANO, (1859-1920), betrayer of the Mexican Revolution, President of Mexico, 1915-1920, and eventual adversary of Emiliano Zapata in Zapata's home state of Morelos where Tepoztlan is located.

LORD OF THE SMOKING MIRROR, Tezcatlipoca, brother of Quetzalcoatl. Of the four sons born of the first principle, Ometeotl, the two god, three of them are called Tezcatlipoca and one Quetzalcoatl. The striving for supremacy between these four gives the universe its dynamic motion, which the Aztecs saw as war, and the divisions of the four ages of time. Tezcatlipoca overthrew the artistic, ascetic, and peace loving period of

Quetzalcoatl thru the use of pulque as the poem relates. This also marks an historical break in the Valley of Mexico after which Tezcatlipoca, the Aztec Huitzilopochtli, and his mystical imperialism, known as the War of the Flowers, acceded to egregious importance. A noble of the calpullis and advisor to Itzeoatl, called Tlacaelel, was the mastermind of this new imperial Aztec state. One of his first acts was the burning of the histories which he then rewrote to align fate and destiny with his "mystic imperialism" which fueled itself with unprecedented quantities of sacrificial blood.

GACHUPIN (Spanish) Derogatory name for the pure blood Spanish used by the Mestizo and Indian people of Mexico.

LORDS OF THE CALPULLI Tecuhtli, (Nahautl), were the heads of the various cognate clans which made up the tribe. Each clan had a totemic designation and organized their habitation in the towns and cities as a semiotic map of the time-space dimensions of the Aztec cosmology.

TEOTL, (Nahautl) literally translated: God. For the linguistic and social analysis of the term which informs my use/abuse of it here, see Huidtfelt, Arild, *Teotl and Ixipilatli.*

XOCHI, (Nahautl) flower; vide Simeon, Remi, *Diccionario de la Nahautl o Mexicana,* Mexico, 1977.

SPARAGMOS, (Greek) dismemberment; associated with sacrificial rites of Dionysius; cf. *The Bacchae.*

XIPE TOTEC, (Nahautl) God of the flayed skin of the sacrificial victims which was worn by the priests: representation wrought to its paradoxical extreme.

COMERCIANTES CRUDOS Y SACROSANTOS, (Spanish) literally translates: (1) merchants (2) raw, uncooked, drunken, rotten, or hungover (3) and (4) sacred, sacrosanct.

CUETES, (Spanish) explosives, fireworks; "vulgar" pronunciation of cohetes.

QUIERO, (Spanish) I want, I desire.

TRAGO, (Spanish) a small drink, usually alcoholic.

LOS DOS VOCES, (Spanish) the two voices.

PLI SELON PLI, (French) fold according to fold. Vide Mallarmé's poem on the appearance of the city of Bruges arising out of the morning mists. cf. Pierre Boulez, *Pli Selon Pli,* Columbia Records, M30296

EJIDOS, (Spanish) public land, commons. In Mexico this refers to the acreage of land which was held and used communally by clans and communities before the encroachment of the great haciendas. The Mexican Revolution was, for the poor farmers of Morelos and elsewhere, a fight for the return of this ancient form of landholding. Much of this land has been returned to the small farming communities like Tepoztlan since the revolution.

"Each loses what he chooses" etc. thru "as I am always talking" and "as mind is a finger pointing" etc. malappropriated with respectful thanks from the work of Robert Creeley, variously and widely, beginning with "Sanine to Leda", *The Charm* thru "I know a man", *For Love,* and "The Finger", *Pieces* and elsewhere.

PUESTO, (Spanish) vendor's stand

"Alas, for flowery mushy, sappy twenty and the sharp Persian sword" from Basil Bunting

LAZARO, (Spanish) a raggedy beggar, body sores, and the biblical figure